BOOK ANALYSIS

Written by Maël Tailler
Translated by Carly Probert

On the Road

BY JACK KEROUAC

Bright Summaries.com

JACK KEROUAC

AMERICAN WRITER

- **Born in Lowell, Massachussetts in 1922**
- **Died in St. Petersburg, Florida in 1969**
- **Notable works:**
  - *On the Road* (1957), novel
  - *Mexico City Blues* (1959), poem
  - *Desolation Angels* (1965), novel

Jack Kerouac was born in Lowell, Massachusetts in 1922. Born to a modest family of French-speaking Canadians, Jean-Louis Kerouac (his birth name) became one of the greatest writers of the Beat generation, along with William Burroughs and Allen Ginsberg.

His novels (*The Dharma Bums*, 1958; *Lonesome Traveller*, 1960; *Big Sur*, 1962) tell of his travels through the United States and criticize the American way of life. Poorly adapted to the stifling social conventions of his time, Kerouac sought his salvation in alcohol, drugs, spirituality (Buddhism) and travelling. A mentor of the American youth in the 1960s, Kerouac died in 1969 from problems related to his alcoholism.

ON THE ROAD

THE TRIBULATIONS OF TWO NON-CONFORMISTS

- **Genre**: autobiographical novel
- **Reference edition:** Kerouac, J. (2003) *On the Road*. New York: Penguin Books.
- **First edition**: 1957
- **Themes**: travel, American society, freedom, marginality, escape

On the Road (1957) tells of the tribulations of Dean Moriarty (Neal Cassady) and Sal Paradise (Kerouac himself), two young hedonistic contrarians, in puritan America of the late 1940s. Travelling the country by hitchhiking, by bus and by car, they embark on a blurred, hectic and existential quest that is sometimes mysterious.

This autobiographical novel, which was reworked several times before its publication, earned its author huge success and is considered one of the most representative works of the Beat generation.

SUMMARY

THE START OF A LONG JOURNEY

Sal Paradise, a lively young college student and apprentice writer, who lives with his aunt in New Jersey, dreams of travelling. He meets a strange character coming from the West, Dean Moriarty. The two men roam the bars of New York philosophizing and plan on meeting again in Denver.

In July 1947, with only $50 in his pocket, Sal embarks on a road trip to escape the grayness of the city and all of its conformity. He is searching for a freer life, which is less subject to the shackles of society. His first trip is a failure, but he sets off again the next day, determined to make a stopover in Denver where his friend is waiting for him. He passes through Chicago, where the bebop (musical trend born in the forties) playing in the bars thrills him. He alternates between hitchhiking from drivers, cowboys, itinerant workers and farmers.

In Denver, Sal stays with his friend Chad in the posh apartment of his friend Tim Gray's parents.

His friend Carlo Marx, a cheeky young college student, phones Sal and invites him to join him. In a basement, Sal finds Dean and Carlo busy with their new hobby: "trying to communicate with absolute honesty and absolute completeness" everything that goes through their heads, with the help of Benzedrine (a type of amphetamine, Part 2, Chapter 7). The trio and some friends spend their evenings partying and talking.

After a trip to the old mining town of Central City, Sal decides to leave the region, accompanied by Rita Betencourt, a "simple and true" girl, with whom he had a brief affair (Part 1, Chapter 10), and travel to San Francisco.

CALIFORNIA, VIRGINIA AND NEW YORK

Sal finds his friend Remi Boncoeur who lives and works in the suburbs of San Francisco as a "special guard" (Part 1, Chapter 11). The idleness of Sal, who spends his days "drinking coffee and scribbling" screenplays for Hollywood, is frowned upon by Remi's girlfriend. He is therefore forced to work with his friend. But when they should be monitoring the barracks visited by the passing sailors, they prefer to drink with them, leaving their posts. The atmosphere at Remi's place deteriorates and Sal decides to leave the same way he arrived: at night and through the window.

In a bus headed to Los Angeles, Sal falls in love with a beautiful Mexican girl, Terry. They spend two weeks together. They try in vain to find work in Hollywood, wandering together along roads and in motels, and staying some time in Sabinal with Terry's family.

Sal ends up finding work as a cotton picker and seems to have reached a balance. But, after making love one last time, he and Terry leave one another without much regret. Sal then resumes his journey. He joins a fascinating hobo for a while ("the Ghost of Susquehanna", Part 1, Chapter 14), reflecting on the dark wildness of the East throughout history, before returning to his aunt's house.

Dean, who has just left his wife, his daughter and his job on a whim, joins Sal at his brother's house in Virginia. Dean is a convinced hedonist (pleasure seeker), who is also in search of more freedom. He bought a car, returned to his former girlfriend, Marylou, and now travels the country with her and Ed Dunkel, a childhood friend who is also fleeing from his wife. The merry group helps Sal's brother to relocate, then returns to New York.

After a short stay interspersed with binge drinking, jazz concerts and excess, they leave for New Orleans, where they meet Old Bull Lee, an educated mystical man, but who is overcome by his heroin addiction. After a few nights of debauchery, they are made to understand that they cannot stay. Dean, Marylou and Sal then hit the road again.

Travelling at full speed through Texas and then California, Dean talks about his difficult childhood with his alcoholic father, who he believes he can recognize in each vagabond. In San Francisco, when they have run out of money, Dean suddenly decides to abandon them to rejoin his wife, Camille.

Sal and Marylou stay together for a while, before she also leaves. Sal, bitter and hungry, finds Camille and Dean, who has become a pressure cooker salesman. Together, they take a lovely walk, then separate, thinking they will never see each other again.

COLORADO, ILLINOIS AND NEW YORK

In spring 1949, Sal returns to Denver but becomes lonely and depressed there. He is nothing more than a "disillusioned white man" (Part 3, Chapter 1). He returns to San Francisco where Dean is failing in his role as a father: he smokes "tea", i.e. marijuana, to the point where he becomes crazy and is still torn between Camille (with whom he argues constantly) and Marylou (who he asks to shoot him). The "two broken-down heroes of the Western night" (Part 3, Chapter 3) plan to leave for Italy with the money that Sal has earned from the publication of his book. Unfortunately, their dream does not come true. After a few evenings with their old friends, the two leave for New York.

Left stranded in Denver by a couple who cannot stand them any longer, they argue and Dean breaks down in tears. The two men, exhausted, make two stopovers.

They go to the tourist office with a stolen car and agree to take a Cadillac full of college students to Chicago. Dean drives like a madman, without sleeping or handing over the wheel, and they arrive at their destination in no time (after a stop at a ranch, swerving off the road and a trip to the police station).

After dropping off the students, Dean and Sal spend the night in bars in Chicago, drinking and dancing. In the morning, they return the Cadillac in a poor state. They then go on as far as Detroit, spend the night in a cinema and hitchhike to New York. Dean meets Inez, a "sexy brunette" (Part 3, Chapter 11), who he gets pregnant and who tries to settle his divorce over the phone with Camille, who has just given birth.

In New York, Dean leads a simple and orderly life: he lives with Inez and works in a parking lot. One night, pondering destiny, speed and the passing of time, Dean says that they might end up "looking in the cans" (Part 4, Chapter 1) and that it could be true freedom. Sal sets off alone to Denver, where he meets some friends including Tim Gray, Ed Dunkel and Stan Shepard. After a festive week in which the old group seems to be back together, Stan, Sal and Dean decide to head south towards Mexico.

MEXICO AND NEW YORK

Despite its poor and tired countryside, Mexico meets their expectations. In Gregoria, they meet Victor who invites them to his home, gives them "tea", then takes them to a brothel. The three men reluctantly leave the city and continue their journey. They eventually reach Mexico, a wild and fascinating city. But shortly after, Sal gets sick. When he wakes up, Stan is gone and Dean is about to do the same.

Sal somehow returns to New York in the fall. There he meets a girl named Laura. Meanwhile, Dean has married Inez, but he left her the same night to join Camille in San Francisco.

One day, on his way home, Sal finds Dean who seems to be destroyed and defeated. A while later, Remi Boncoeur (now a "fat and sad" bourgeois, Part 5) invites Sal and Laura to attend a Duke Ellington concert, but he refuses to invite Dean. So, they leave him sad and alone on a street corner. Later,

Sal is meditating on a dock in New Jersey: he remembers his travels and gives a special thought to Dean Moriarty (who he never saw) and his father (who they never found).

CHARACTER STUDY

SAL PARADISE (THE NARRATOR)

The author hides behind this pseudonym in this autobiographical novel. Sal is also an abbreviation of Salvatore ("the savior" in Italian) and Paradise refers to the hero's idealism when he leaves for the West (and the South) to seek a freer life (the lost paradise of his generation).

This apprentice writer (who readily quotes Dostoevsky, London, Steinbeck and Céline) hits the road accompanied by Dean to escape the dullness and conformity he sees in New York (he lives with his aunt in New Jersey). Like Dean, he is an adventurer and bon vivant who loves the night, traveling, partying and meeting new people, but he remains constantly under the excesses of his friend (for example, as witnessed by his shyness during his sexual relations with Marylou, or by his relatively safe driving). Passive and dominated, he willingly allows himself to be led by Dean, but still retains his critical stance.

DEAN MORIARTY

This character (directly inspired by a friend of Kerouac, Neal Cassady) forms, along with Sal Paradise (the author's double) the main duo in *On the Road*.

Dean, with his long sideburns (Part 1, Chapter 1), systematically stained or torn clothes and sloppy appearance, embodies the bad boy. He had a difficult childhood with an alcoholic father, then in a correctional facility. He is a marginal with a tendency to drinking and drugs, but he is not really dangerous or violent.

Sal considers him a mentor. He is hedonistic, as well as nonconformist, and an unwavering optimist (his motto is "Yes! Yes! Yes"). He is always searching for new adventures and freedom. He is also an unfaithful husband and an irresponsible father. Disowned by most of his friends, he will end up miserable and alone. However, the novel (and Kerouac's work in general) constantly celebrates this type of marginality as a higher degree of freedom. Dean embodies, more than madness or eccentricity, a certain holiness.

CARLO MARX

His name refers directly to Karl Marx, giving a nod to Allen Ginsberg's political beliefs (American poet and friend of Kerouac, 1926-1997), but is also reminiscent of the Marx Brothers. A cheeky college student, he devotes himself to poetry and philosophy. He remains quieter and away from the main duo.

Good to know: Characters 'à clef'

We speak of a 'roman à clef' (French meaning 'novel with a key') and characters à clef when, as in *On the Road*, the characters refer to real people, more or less explicitly.

Karl Marx was a German philosopher, economist and writer (1818-1883). With Friedrich Engels, he developed the Theory of Revolutionary Proletarian Socialism and wrote *The Communist Manifesto*. He criticized capitalism and predicted its collapse. Today, we speak of Marxism to describe the trend that followed the ideas of this politician.

The Marx Brothers: these were American comic actors who played for cinema, television and the theater until the 1950s. Groucho, Harpo, Chico, Gummo and Zeppo were actually brothers.

OLD BULL LEE (WILLIAM BURROUGHS)

This marginal academic, a follower of all drugs, leads a dissolute and contrasted life (he married a Yugoslav countess, was an exterminator in Chicago, etc.) before retiring with his girlfriend (Jane) in New Orleans.

He becomes a mystic and a heroin addict, and henceforth seeks knowledge through drugs. His ambivalent name is both a reference to a fictional Indian chief and a fierce opponent of the Washington bureaucracy during the American Civil War (conflict about the Black Question, from 1861 to 1865), General Lee.

REMI BONCOEUR

Remi Boncoeur (whose real name is Henri Cru) is a childhood friend of Sal who went to live in San Francisco. His trajectory reflects that of many other characters in the book: he is a bon vivant seeking adventures to "settle down" quickly.

He marries Ann Lee (who has "a bad tongue" and comes "from a small town in Oregon", Part 1, Chapter 11), before abandoning his tumultuous life and becoming a "fat and sad" bourgeois man (Part 5).

THE WOMEN

Sal and Dean meet many women during their journey. This is also one of the reasons why they decide to embark on a trip. Although recurrent, women nevertheless play a secondary role which is often presented as negative (by the narrator). Camille, Marylou and Inez, for example, try in vain to normalize Dean, and Sal cannot help but see them as obstacles to his adventure.

Sal has several affairs (Terry, the young Mexican girl, Babe Rawlins, "the doll from the West", Rita, a "simple and true" girl (Part 1, Chapter 10), Marylou, Laura, etc.), but systematically refuses any lasting relationship. They are generally considered (from a self-aware, macho point of view) as objects of desire and not as interesting interlocutors. They are nevertheless an essential part of the lifestyle claimed by Sal and Dean.

ANALYSIS

BEAT GENERATION, COUNTER-CULTURE AND AMERICAN SOCIETY

Beat Generation

The term 'beat' refers to the distress of the young American generation after the Second World War. It also refers to rhythm and pulse, as the 'beatniks' were huge fans of jazz.

The Beat Generation thus refers to a literary and cultural movement that developed in the United States in the fifties and sixties. Its main members (Kerouac, Burroughs, Ginsberg) showed their rejection of industrial and McCarthyism society which they opposed with spirituality (Zen Buddhism), travels and drug-induced experiences. They profoundly influenced the culture of the twentieth century.

GOOD TO KNOW: MCCARTHYISM

McCarthyism (named after US Senator Joseph McCarthy, 1908-1957) indicates a political persecution and sidelining of any person suspected of being Communist in America in the fifties. Implemented in a climate of psychosis, in the context of the Cold War (1945-1990), it became a real "witch hunt".

A criticism of society

In his novel, Kerouac is engaged in a constant criticism of

American post-war society. It is not a systematic argument, but scattered portraits, descriptions and reflections as they come across new cities, situations and people. Sal and Dean emphasize:

- The stupidity and arrogance of the police, as well as the limits and dangers of militarism (the novel namely evokes the invention of the hydrogen bomb, Part 4, Chapter 6);
- The illusion of happiness and well-being in civilization, and the feeling of belonging to a "screwed generation";
- Puritanism, the foolish conformism, and the complacency of the middle class ("the absurd devices it had fallen to keep its proud tradition", Part 1, Chapter 4), the collegians and the bourgeois;
- The boredom inherent to an individualist, materialistic, hyper-secure, standardized and meaningless way of life;
- The coldness and negativity of the East Coast intellectuals;
- The racism against blacks (often relegated to lower functions) and the Mexicans, as well as the growing McCarthyism;
- The cruel inequalities that brutally manifest themselves in large cities.

Counter-culture

Kerouac, relatively disillusioned in relation to the history and evolution of society, defends smaller utopias rather than an anti-conformist way of life and of thinking. This lifestyle is characterized by:

- The absolute hunger for freedom that sometimes grows

to ignore the law (speeding, drunk driving, car theft, drug use, etc.). It is therefore a form of anarchism, although not activism;
- The rejection of the American dream, this double illusion of believing that the accumulation of material goods will necessarily lead to happiness and that, regardless of social background or skin color, we can all get to the top of the social pyramid;
- An open mind and boundless curiosity;
- A cult of marginality and a certain madness as a direct response to castrating conformism, and the attraction to the marginals (particularly hobos) and minorities;
- An unwavering optimism, warm and generous, that can face any adversity;
- Passionate hedonism (eating well, drinking, taking drugs, partying, dancing, laughing, sexual pleasure, enjoying every moment, even bordering on excess);
- A constant escapism (through incessant travel, alcohol and drugs) from the daily reality and the frozen gaze that "normality" imposes.

These lifestyle choices are obviously not safe. At the end of the novel, Sal seems disoriented and bitter, Old Bull Lee sinks into his addiction, and Dean, prematurely aged, is rejected by everyone and destined to a life of wandering and misery, but without the energy or optimism of youth. Some writers of the Beat Generation (Kerouac and Ginsberg, among others) have experienced this kind of epilogue themselves.

FLOW, MOVEMENT AND SPEED POETICS

The journey made by Sal and Dean, even though it can be divided into different trips and though they do not always go in the same direction, gives the impression of a single stream of events, symbolized by the road. They also explicitly compare the road to human destiny. In addition, the protagonists repeatedly pass through the same locations (particular Denver) as if their movement were cyclical.

Dean is literally obsessed with the idea of movement. On the road, as in life, he never wants to stop, and rather than speed (a characteristic value of modern life in the West) Dean is searching for an adequate pace for the events. He finds the expression of this pace in the music of the African-American jazz musicians and develops his theory of "IT". The "IT" is, in a way, what every musician is looking for, the precise and sacred moment when the soloist is able to crystallize the best of himself in communion with the audience that is listening carefully, and realizes that something indefinable and magic is happening. Kerouac also interprets the term 'beatnik' in this way: 'beat' becomes 'be at it', being 'with', having the 'it', according to Bernard Nouis.

This interest in movement takes several forms in the writing.

Material support

Originally, *On the Road* was in the form of a continuous roll of paper that measured 35 meters in length, without divisions (chapters or parts) and with minimal punctuation. The author claims to have typed it out in three weeks, in one surge (Kerouac therefore had to redraft the text several times before it was published). Thus, we find the idea of continuous flow in the physical medium of the work.

Narration

The narrator leads the reader into a flow of words: reflections, portraits, biographies, anecdotes and reports keep coming, mingle and refer to each other like the moving thoughts of a man, like his associations of ideas.

It is not strictly an interior monologue (since the narrator includes stories of other characters, and since he distances himself from the story by anticipating certain events or looking back at them). But the different sequences, overloaded with events, result in a series of sentences that are relatively short, usually juxtaposed and uncoordinated:

> "We hurried back to our miner's shack. Everything was in preparation for the big party. The girls, Babe and Betty, cooked up a snack of beans and franks, and then we danced and started on the beer for fair. The opera over, great crowds of young girls came piling into our place. Rawlins and Tim and I licked our lips. We grabbed them and danced. There was no music, just dancing. The place filled up. People began to bring bottles. We rushed out to hit the bars and rushed back. The night was getting more and more frantic. I wished Dean and Carlo were there-then I realized they'd be out of place and unhappy. They were like the man with the dungeon stone and the gloom, rising from the underground, the sordid hipsters of America, a new beat generation that I was slowly joining" (Part 1, Chapter 9).

The way in which Dean expresses himself (sometimes in direct speech) is also significant and accentuates the impression of speed and the movement of thought described above:

> "'Why, Sa-a-al!' said Dean. 'Well now-ah-ahem-yes, of course, you've arrived-you old sonumbitch you finally got on that old road. Well, now, look here-we must-yes, yes, at once-we must, we really must! Now Camille-' And he swirled on her. 'Sal is here, this is my old buddy from New Yor-r-k, this is his first night in Denver and it's absolutely necessary for me to take him out and fix him up with a girl'" (Part 1, Chapter 7).

Ellipses

Other formal events are used to create this impression of speed, such as ellipses (time hopping).

Around the notions of flow, motion and speed, Kerouac seems to have wanted to express, in the most appropriate and accurate way, a happy and intense period of his life.

FURTHER REFLECTION

- Some characters in the novel are 'characters à clef'. Explain what this means.
- How are women represented in the novel? Do you agree with this perspective?
- What characterizes the Beat Generation? How are the characters in the novel representative of this generation?
- Through his work, what does Kerouac criticize?
- In your opinion, is Kerouac a revolutionary? Does he seek to improve society? Justify your answer.
- Do the characters in the novel have a purpose in their lives? What are they looking for?
- What does the road symbolize?
- In your opinion, why did the author first publish his work in the form of a 35-meter long roll of paper?
- How can we explain Kerouac's interest in movement and speed?

We want to hear from you!
Leave a comment on your online library
and share your favourite books on social media!

FURTHER READING

REFERENCE EDITION

- Kerouac, J. (2003) *On the Road*. New York: Penguin Books.

ADAPTATIONS

- *On the Road*. (2002) [Film]. Walter Salles. Dir.
- *On the Road*. (2005) [Radio drama]. Christine Bernard-Sugy. Dir.